Must be This Tall to Ride

Stephanie Parris

BookLeaf
Publishing

India | USA | UK

Presentation by *BookLeaf Publishing*

Web: www.bookleafpub.com

E-mail: info@bookleafpub.com

ISBN: 9789360944896

First edition 2024

Scrolling on Instagram at 3am

Some people have no chill
I am one of them
Your earrings are skeleton hands
Please take me to the grave
You have green eyes
I'll drink your crocodile tears
You have messy hair
Let me be the one to give you bed head
I'll make you biscuits and gravy from scratch
I'm trying to undig myself from this hole
But it's been at least 30 years
I'm going to need a grace period
Don't let me get hit by a bus

I Got Loneliness as a Pet (Should have got a Bearded Dragon)

Loneliness lives with me
Lying beneath my bedsheets
Between the pages of my book
Existing in the steam from my hot shower
I write messages about it
On fogged mirrors
Loneliness gives breath to my exhales with such ease
How it delights in taking the air out of my lungs
While I struggle and gasp to suck in and breathe
Like a living thing, loneliness curls up in the space between my ribs
A faint purring, thrumming against my bones
Alone, alone, alone, alone, alone, alone
And how I ache fiercely to be seen, to be held
But a soft growl reminds me I am not meant for such pleasures

Broken Bones can be Poetry too

Living, breathing filth
Human garbage
Someone take me out
To the dumpster
Light a match and drop it
Let me burnnnnn

You can't dress up trash
Only take it out
Somebody take me out
No holy water can save me now
Open my mouth, spit, swallow
Let it burn my throat

Maybe all my skin will fall off
The flesh will peel back
And I'll be Left with a skeleton
Broken bones can be poetry too

6/23/23

I keep waiting
Thinking today's the day
That life will be too heavy
But I keep waking up
My lungs keep inhaling
Heart keeps pumping
My body is a traitor
Or maybe my savior
Today we keep going

Unrequited

Becoming my muse
Was the worst and best thing
You ever did to me

Praying for a Comedian

Though the Gods are cruel
They have a sense of humor
One can only hope the same of Karma
Perhaps she has jokes
Because after all
If we're not laughing, we're crying
And if we're not living, we're dying

A Four Year Affair

His favorite color was orange
Like the sun
How fitting
I laugh while I spend another year
Rotating around him

Home Sweet Home

I ache
Bones crumbling underneath
Paper thin skin
How do you wear your heart on your sleeve
When it's all dried up
Veins full of dust
Cut me open
Bring a broom and dust pan to the hospital
Breathing has always been difficult
Each inhale is a reminder of what could have
been
And every exhale brings me closer to a final
resting ground
Dance around the elephant in the room
The girl digging her grave in the kitchen
Fingers in the blender, head in the oven
No one was ever going to stay

Wanting To Forget You

I patiently wait for the day
When I wake up and I don't have anything
Left to write about us

When it's all been thought of
And all been said
When he's no longer my muse
And I'm not followed by memories

But until then
I'll wake up, tucked in white sheets
Wearing his tshirt
Dreaming of late nights
Being held in arms
With half finished tattoos

Burn Me Alive

Hands delicately grip the knife
Muscles tense in your tanned forearms
What I would do
To waltz in your veins
Thrumming with your blood
Dip my head back
Drag your tongue across my neck
Suck every earring out of my lobe
Give me a reason to come back
To come
Across tongues that are twisted
Let me be bittersweet

And how tragic, the more I thought of us
The more I burned
Yet I didn't feel combustible
The flames engulfed all else
I'd rebuild an entire civilization over ashes
Let the smoke settle in my lungs
Unraveling in the heat
Melting my brain
You pray to the Gods for a flood
I was born hot blooded and finally felt it

Second Best

Don't mind my wear and tear
A little rough around the edges
I could be your second best
Happy to be your silver lining
Gold never looked good on me anyway

White Sheets

His hands twisted in my hair
Pulling my head back
I grasp the pillows
Tangled in white sheets
I adore the way he looks in white
And I love the way he leaves me with bruises
His hands wrap around my throat
And I don't care if I ever breathe again

I am The Lighthouse and The Siren

A man once called me a lighthouse
Believing I had a light inside of me
Another called me a callous harlot
Sucking the soul out of men
I think I am both
The creator and the destroyer
It's always been on borrowed time
At birth the umbilical cord wrapped too tight
Over before it began
Struggling for breath before I knew how to
inhale
22 years later the cancer spread
Still I danced out of a skeleton grasp
Feet skipping over grave stones
Reality tumbling down
But I've been treading water since day one
The crashing waves a comforting lullaby
Salty tears, desperate gasps, toss me around
I romanticized being someone else for so long
That I fear I no longer know who I am

I've Never had Much of a Green Thumb

I have never so desperately desired to be
someone else
To exist within a stranger's walls
To be called by another's name
A sweet embrace of something not me
And reader, before you scold me
Before you remind me "the grass isn't always
greener on the other side"
I fear it's never going to be green for me
Regardless of how much I water it
So let me be caressed by such tender thoughts
Of being anyone else aside from myself

Broken Parts

You never asked me to feel this much
As if I wanted this
As if it were a faucet I could simply turn
Or a light I could gently flip
Yet here I am blinded and slowly drowning

Revelations

I could hear the crows coming for me
They waited in the parking lot
As I left the air conditioned grocery store
God sent them
He knew I was barren

The Reality

Drove by a neighborhood tonight
A neighborhood we drove through
Last December, looking at Christmas lights
Now it's March
And I'm rotting in a hotel room

A blur of choices brought me here
Everything feels tasteless now
When your best isn't good enough
And the problem is you
It's hard to swallow

Let me bleed out on the sidewalks
Paint this city red with my blood
I'll never come back home
There will never be a me with you

White sheets aren't so white anymore
Maybe it was never cute to toss and turn
Cabernet makes me nauseous
The window seat makes me feel like a whore
Saying Sorry feels like a cop out

My Karma had a Name

I knew karma was coming
But I didn't know he'd be so attractive
So inviting
I didn't know he'd be charming
Handsome with strong hands
A jawline you could lick from lip to ear
Eyes so green,
you saw entire national forests in them
Someone to over indulge in
Happily drunk on every ounce of them
But so utterly rotten to the core
So shallow that when you dive into them
You hit rock bottom
I deserve this
I deserve you

He Likes Me, He Likes Me Not

I wanted to like the way you smelled on me
In my hair and on my skin
I never wanted to be black or white
But being grey is so much worse
Limbo is endless
A slow burn
And I have enough kindling to last lifetimes

But then you had to go
And make me a cliche
Writing about a boy
Who looks dangerously attractive
Smoking cigarettes
With a smirk that drips of sarcasm
A voice that rumbles with gravel
In the darkness of his room

If the statue of David
Contained molten rage and eternal springs
You'd make Michelangelo envious
You will always be art to me

Hurt People, Hurt People

I kept waiting for the earth to split
To swallow me whole
Laying down on my back
Like I had my entire life
But the ground isn't ready for me yet

My therapist told me
"Hurt people, hurt people"
And there's no one I hurt more than myself

I would like to meet the woman I've become
With arms wide open
To make her feel seen, heard, loved, safe
I've spent most of my life hating who I am
But I can still be who I want to be
Who I said I would be

To Kill Myself

How long had I been here
Pulling and stretching at my skin
Biting cuticles until they bled
Grinding down my bones
Clenching my jaw
Eyes squeezed shut
Gagging on the shame
The relentless waves of criticism
Tonight I let them break over me
Lick the salt off of my lips
I'm finding my way back to my body
Finger tips brush my throat
Recalling the sound of my voice
The warmth of my blood

Slowly peeling off the husk of who I was
I let the tide swallow her
And Carry her out to sea

How stirring it is
To kill yourself
Only to find life again